Journey into Wholeness

Steps to Emotional Wholeness

Healing the Wounds of Abuse

companion to:
Journey into Wholeness DVD series
and Traveling with the Life-Giver

Carol Romeo

AuthorHouse™
1663 Liberty Drive
Bloomington, IN 47403
www.authorhouse.com
Phone: 1 (800) 839-8640

Published by AuthorHouse 07/28/2015

ISBN: 978-1-4969-5736-8 (sc)
ISBN: 978-1-4969-5737-5 (e)

Scripture references (unless otherwise noted) are taken from the Spirit-Filled Life Bible,
New King James Version, Copyright © 1991 by Thomas Nelson, Inc.

Scriptures marked NLT are taken from the Life Recovery Bible, New Living Translation,
Copyright © by Tyndale House Publishers, Inc., Wheaton, IL 60189

Print information available on the last page.

Any people depicted in stock imagery provided by Dreamstime are models,
and such images are being used for illustrative purposes only.
Certain stock imagery © Dreamstime.

This book is printed on acid-free paper.

authorHOUSE®

Contents

Dedication

I dedicate this writing to my beloved Lord Jesus Christ. Thank you for the gifts you have given me and the abundance of your love and grace you have poured upon me. This is my humble attempt at giving back to you as I give out to others in need. You have said,

> *"Then the King will say to those on His right hand, 'Come, you blessed of My Father, inherit the kingdom prepared for you from the foundation of the world: for I was hungry and you gave Me food; I was thirsty and you gave Me drink; I was a stranger and you took me in; I was naked and you clothed Me; I was sick and you visited Me; I was in prison and you came to Me.'*

> *"Then the righteous will answer Him, saying, 'When did we see You a stranger and take You in, or naked and clothe You? Or when did we see You sick, or in prison, and come to You?' "And the King will answer and say to them, 'Assuredly, I say to you, inasmuch as you did it to one of the least of these My brethren, you did it to Me (Matthew 25:34-40).'*

Thank you all for giving me this opportunity to serve you. I pray that you receive all that Jesus has purposed for you to receive through this writing and, at the Lord's command, *give what you receive.*

Introduction

Hi, my name is Carol Romeo and I want to welcome all of you to my teaching series: *Journey into Wholeness*. This workbook is designed for use in conjunction with the DVD series: *Journey into Wholeness*, and my book, *Traveling with the Life-Giver*. I am a licensed Marriage and Family Therapist as well as holding a master's degree in Practical Ministry. My heart (as you will see in my teaching) is to combine the spiritual with psychological tools to better facilitate your healing. I will share what I have learned from my own healing and recovery as well as what I have discovered in my work with others.

Because of my own prior abuse—abuse is a specialty that kind-of landed in my lap. I don't know if you have heard the statement, "God takes our mess and turns it into our life-message?" Well, that is exactly what Jesus did for me. If you are suffering, my heart breaks for you because I know what it feels like. But, you are in the right place if you are making yourself available for God to do something new in your life.

It is my desire that you will gain strength, direction and the tools that you need for your journey towards wholeness through this teaching series. It is best experienced with others in a group or at least find a partner to go through the series with you. We are reminded in James 5:16, "Confess your sins to each other and pray for each other so that you may be healed." I like to remember the statement, "We are harmed in relationship and we are also healed in relationship."

This series is designed as an eight-week study with an introduction teaching. You will read (at home) a chapter a week from *Traveling with the Life-Giver* and answer the questions at the end of each chapter. When you come together you can watch the DVD teaching for that week and break up in groups to share your responses to the questions in *Traveling with the Life-Giver*. Included in the DVD series are several personal testimonies, which can expand your picture of how big your God really is. Truly, there is no wound, which is out of His ability to heal.

I pray God's blessings on you as you take this step to expand your emotional, mental, spiritual and relational health. I want to remind you that you are right where God wants you to be in this time and place. Try not to compare your progress with the progress of others. God is ready to meet you right now today.

Introduction
What is Abuse?

What is Abuse?

- *Any mistreatment* of another person inflicting physical, sexual or emotional harm (intentional or unintentional)

- Treatment that affects the *well-being* of the other individual (ex. Not attending to feeding and bathing a child or elder adult)

All forms of abuse cause emotional scaring

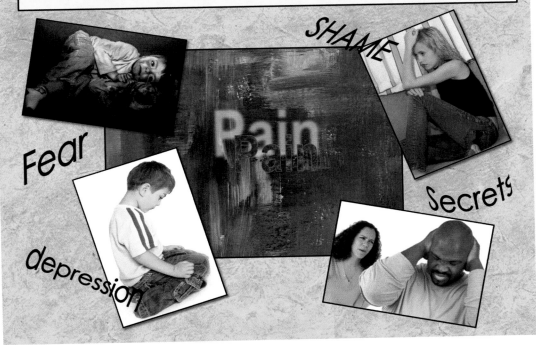

SHAME

Fear

Pain

Secrets

depression

The worse kind of abuse is in the home!

◆ Children (*especially small children*) require safety and protection from the parent in order to thrive.

◆ *Early childhood wounds* can produce severe pathology because the higher cognitive functions are not developed as yet.

Abuse
Damages
the
Whole
Individual!

Testimony

_____

_____

_____

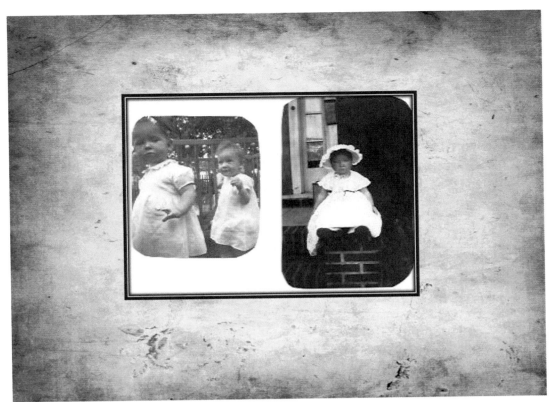

_____

_____

_____

_____

In Reality

Abuse Damages the Whole Individual!

Victim Profile = I AM UNSAFE

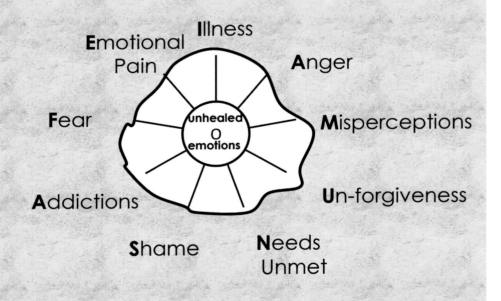

Illness

Emotional Pain

Anger

Fear

Misperceptions

unhealed O emotions

Un-forgiveness

Addictions

Shame

Needs Unmet

Chapter One
Leaving the Kingdom

Loss of Direction

- Cherished makes the poor choice to leave Life-Giver and travel alone into the unknown territory outside of His kingdom.

- She lost sight of His love.

- Her anger at His perceived abandonment drove her in the wrong direction.

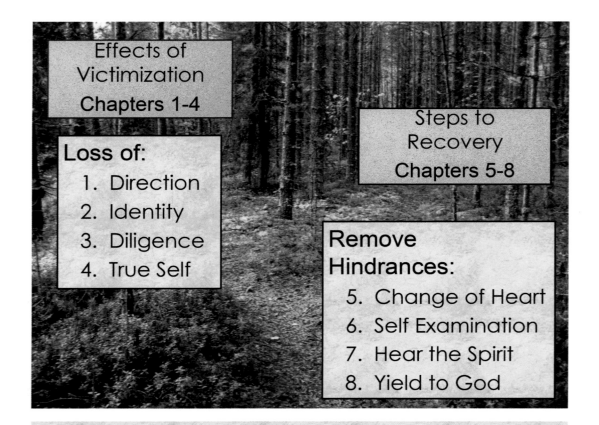

Effects of Victimization
Chapters 1-4

Loss of:
1. Direction
2. Identity
3. Diligence
4. True Self

Steps to Recovery
Chapters 5-8

Remove Hindrances:
5. Change of Heart
6. Self Examination
7. Hear the Spirit
8. Yield to God

Assess your strengths and weaknesses

- Is your environment safe?
- Are your physical needs met?
- Do you have external supports?
- Are you acting out in an addiction?
- What is your internal strength like?
- Any mental or emotional illness?

_____

_____

_____

> Cherished forgot the promises. Her thoughts and behaviors were being ruled by her emotional wounds.

Emotions are Leading

SOUL
↓
BODY
↓
SPIRIT

Automatic Response	God Empowered Response
1. Fear	1. Peace
2. Powerlessness	2. Empowerment
3. Out of Control	3. Confidence
4. Insecure	4. Safe in God
5. Helplessness	5. Knowledge of choices
6. Anger	6. Acceptance
7. Mistrust	7. Trust
8. Panic	8. Rest
9. Anxiety	9. Flow
10. Dissociation (Disconnection)	10. Connection (body & emotions)
11. Hopelessness	11. Hope / Faith
12. Despair	12. Move towards life

_____

_____

_____

_____

Seven Steps to Successful Emotional Management

1. Learn to feel or *experience* the emotion:

- Damaged emotions can be rediscovered
- Experiencing our emotions is crucial to understanding and managing them

2. Recognize the emotion you are experiencing:

- Learn how to identify and label what you are feeling

- Rate the intensity from 1-10

_____

_____

_____

3. Assess the root cause of the emotion:

Is the trigger?

- A past situation
- A present situation or
- A present situation triggered by a past emotion?

4. Gain the ability to experience pleasant and unpleasant emotions without under or over reacting.

✓ This ability, to a great extent, has to do with a learned capacity for containment.

✓ People who have suffered trauma may find this task difficult.

✓ Containment can be learned through journaling the emotions or talking with a trusted other.

5. Learn how to self-soothe:

- Learn how to bring yourself down if upset or aroused.

6. Look at your possible options for expressing your emotions:

- What, if anything, do you want the other person to know?

- Journal, write letters that you don't send, role play or discuss your options with others.

7. Make a conscious choice to act!

- What behavior is appropriate and will convey what you feel?

- Your action needs to come from a conscious decision.

_____

_____

_____

Seven Steps to Successful Emotional Management

1. Learn to feel or experience the emotion.

2. Recognize the emotions you are experiencing.

3. Assess the root cause of the emotion.

4. Gain the ability to experience pleasant and unpleasant emotions without under or over reacting.

5. Learn how to self-soothe.

6. Look at your options for expressing your emotions.

7. Make a choice to act.

Carol Romeo
2007

Self-Awareness Chart

Date	Situation	Feelings	Automatic Thoughts	Realistic Answers	Outcome
	What were you doing? With whom? What was the inter-action?	Label the emotion and rate the intensity 1-10.	What is the negative belief (s) about your-self or the situation?	What evidence does not support that belief? Ask God for the truth.	What are you feeling now? Rate the intensity 1-10.

"Be anxious for nothing, but in everything by prayer and supplication, with thanksgiving, let your requests be known to God; and the peace of God, which surpasses all understanding, will guard your hearts and minds through Christ Jesus."

Philippians 4:6-7

Use the self-awareness chart and work with one feeling that you can recall:

Date	Situation	Feelings	Automatic Thoughts	Realistic Answers	Outcome
	What were you doing? With whom? What was the inter-action?	Label the emotion and rate the intensity 1-10.	What is the negative belief (s) about your-self or the situation?	What evidence does not support that belief? Ask God for the truth.	What are you feeling now? Rate the intensity 1-10.

_____

_____

_____

Chapter Two
Entering the Valley of Despair

Loss of Identity

- Without Life-Giver and His loving presence, Cherished felt *discarded*.

- She could not retain the *identity* He gave her as His child and adopted the name Forsaken.

- Cherished believed the *lie* of the enemy that she was bad and *shameful*.

God Created Human Beings with Legitimate and Pure Needs and Longings

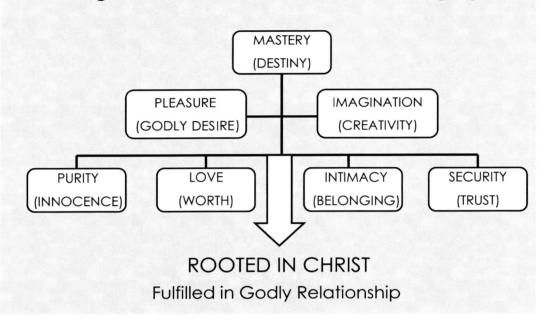

```
                    ┌──────────────┐
                    │   MASTERY    │
                    │  (DESTINY)   │
                    └──────┬───────┘
          ┌────────────────┤
  ┌───────────────┐  ┌─────────────────┐
  │   PLEASURE    │  │   IMAGINATION   │
  │(GODLY DESIRE) │  │  (CREATIVITY)   │
  └───────────────┘  └─────────────────┘
┌──────────┐ ┌────────┐ ┌────────────┐ ┌────────────┐
│  PURITY  │ │  LOVE  │ │  INTIMACY  │ │  SECURITY  │
│(INNOCENCE)│ │(WORTH) │ │(BELONGING) │ │  (TRUST)   │
└──────────┘ └────────┘ └────────────┘ └────────────┘
```

ROOTED IN CHRIST
Fulfilled in Godly Relationship

Mastery
Destiny

Pleasure
Godly Desire

Imagination
Creativity

Purity
Innocence

Intimacy
Belonging

Love
Worth

Security
Trust

Secure Self

_____

_____

_____

Human Needs and Longings Corrupted

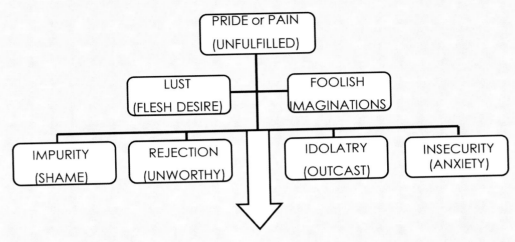

ROOTED IN THE WORLD
Wounded in Sinful Relationship

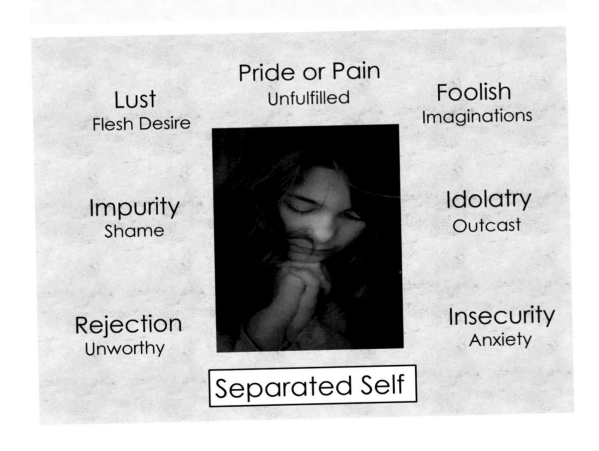

Secure Attachment

Parental Behavior

- Parent is emotionally available: predictable, sensitive and attuned

- Parent shows interest in and aligns with the states of mind of the child

- Parent is perceptive and responsive: he/she is able to repair ruptures

- Pays attention to the God given longings and needs of the child

Child as Adult

- They value relationships

- Can integrate past, present and future (make sense of life history)

- Have an autonomous or free state of mind with respect to attachment

- Their God given longings and needs are met and they can fulfill their destiny

Healthy Relational Attachments

- God created human beings with legitimate and pure basic needs and longings.

- Our needs and longings are to be nurtured and fulfilled within relationships.

- We are harmed in relationship.

- We are also healed in relationship.

> Shame entered the human experience when sin entered.

> "Then the eyes of both of them were opened, and they knew that they were naked; and they sewed fig leaves together and made themselves coverings...and Adam and his wife hid themselves from the presence of the Lord God among the trees of the garden."
>
> **Genesis 3:7&8**

Human Needs and Longings Corrupted

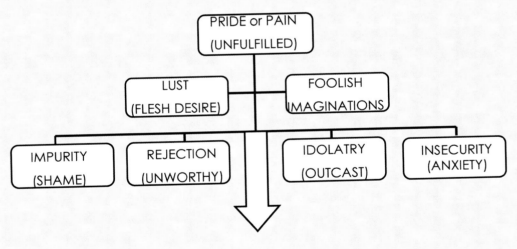

ROOTED IN THE WORLD
Wounded in Sinful Relationship

Dysfunctional Attachment Patterns

Avoidant Attachment

- *Distant emotionally*

- *Low affect attunement*

- *Insensitive to child's needs*

Ambivalent Attachment

- *Inconsistent availability, sensitivity or effectiveness*

- *Parent is either preoccupied with self or intrudes own emotions onto the child.*

_____

_____

_____

Disorganized Attachment

- *Parent has extreme shifts of emotions and behaviors.*

- *Interactions are frightening and confusing to the child.*

- *The parental message is, "come here, go away."*

Wounds are the result

- Through abuse and/or neglect the needs and longings ordained by God are left unmet and perverted.

- Which can lead an individual to believe that:

  ✔ There is something wrong with me (*shame*)
  ✔ There is something wrong with my needs (*I should not have any*)
  ✔ I have to meet my needs any way I can (*false self / perverted need.*)

Shame / Guilt

- Shame is destructive because the message that shame gives is: "I am bad."

- Guilt says, "I did a bad thing." When we truly sin, we need to receive forgiveness; but, we also need to change our ways.

- When we are suffering from false shame, we need to take in God's grace and change the self-condemning lies.

Wounded Heart Cycle

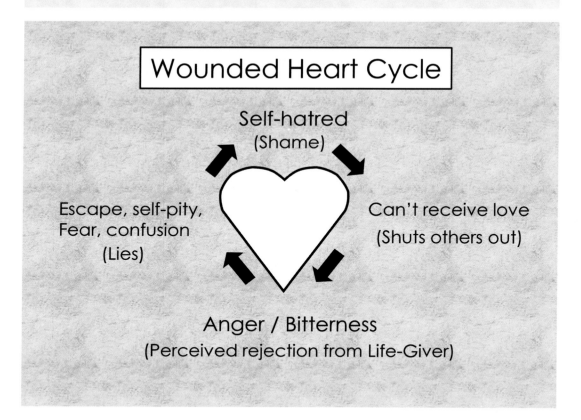

Self-hatred
(Shame)

Can't receive love
(Shuts others out)

Escape, self-pity,
Fear, confusion
(Lies)

Anger / Bitterness
(Perceived rejection from Life-Giver)

When we are wounded we are vulnerable to several different voices *guiding* us:

- Satan and the demonic

- Our own inner wounds speaking to us

- Other people

Cherished lost her sense of identity when she believed the lies!

- She failed to see herself as Cherished and embraced her new identity, Forsaken.

- Cherished acted out of her shame and withdrew from the love she previously experienced with Life-Giver.

- Because she was abandoned by her parents, she believed that Life-Giver also abandoned her. (Lie)

"For the Spirit teaches you all things, and what he teaches is true—it is not a lie. So continue in what he has taught you, and continue to live in Christ."

I John 2:27b NLT

_____

_____

_____

Lie	→	Truth

Lie	Truth
I'm too vulnerable	He is my hiding place (Psalm 32:7)
I am worthless	I am chosen, a royal priesthood (1 Peter 2:9)
I am shameful	I will forget the shame of my youth (Isaiah 54:4)
I am forgotten	He will not forget me (Isaiah 49:15)
I am abandoned	He will not abandon me (Deuteronomy 4:31)
I am alone	His faithful love will be with me (Psalm 89:24)
Only bad comes to me	The Lord is good to all (Psalm 145:9)
God doesn't hear me	He is near to all who call on Him (Psalm 145:18)
I've blown it for too long	He is patient with me (2 Peter 3:9)
I am fearful	I will have nothing to fear (Isaiah 54:14)
I am anxious	The Lord blesses me with peace (Psalm 29:11)
I am grieved	He turns my mourning into gladness (Jeremiah 31:13)
I have to be perfect	It is by grace I am saved (Ephesians 2:8)
I am powerless to change	His strength is perfected in weakness (2 Cor.12:9)
I can't forgive myself	He forgives all my sins (Psalm 103:3)
I can't forgive others	I can forgive because He forgave me (Ephesians 4:32)
I am hated	My enemies are at peace with me (Proverbs 16:7)
I am broken	He will heal my wounded heart (Psalm 147:3)
I am hopeless	My hope comes from Him (Psalm 62:5)
I have no future	The Lord plans for my future (Jeremiah 29:11)
I am distressed	He comforts me in all my trouble (2 Corinthians 1:4)

What are the lies you have believed?
What truth do you need to apply?

- Lie _____
- Truth _____

- Lie _____
- Truth _____

- Lie _____
- Truth _____

_____
_____
_____

Chapter Three
Opposing Forces

Loss of Diligence

Lacked Diligence

- In spite of the Spirit's attempts to strengthen Forsaken and give her vision, she continued to **spiral down** in her emotions.

- In her **depleted state** she lacked the ability to attend to Life-Giver's goal for her.

- Forsaken felt **powerless** to over-come the elements around her.

_____

_____

_____

Unattended Wounds
Downward Spiral

Wound
Emotional distress
Lack of coping skills
Acting out behavior
Guilt/shame
Emotional withdrawal
Defenses fail
Out of control
Powerlessness
Fear
Despair
Breakdown

Toni Tomlinson

TESTIMONY

Come out of denial

- Hopeless about the future
- A string of failed relationships
- Lack of connection with others
- Feel low most of the time
- Nervous and on-edge
- No sense of purpose
- Negative thoughts intrude often
- Panic when asserting self
- Feel unsafe
- Addiction or self-defeating behavior
- Feelings of inadequacy or low self-worth
- Poor attention span
- Thoughts of dying
- Cry often or not at all
- Feel numb
- Frequent anger
- Fear of what others' think

Don't Ignore the Signs!

What are your warning signs?

_____

_____

_____

 # Make a choice to open your eyes!

These are the warning signs I see in my life:

_____

My wounds are:

_____

Here is where I am on the downward spiral:

_____

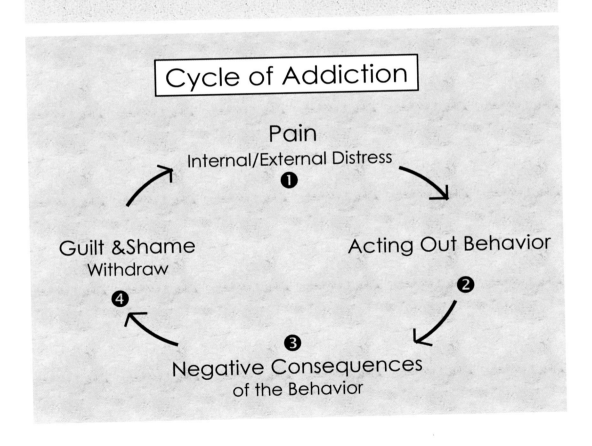

Cycle of Addiction

Pain
Internal/External Distress
❶

Acting Out Behavior
❷

Negative Consequences
of the Behavior
❸

Guilt &Shame
Withdraw
❹

_____

_____

_____

Come to Me

Come to Me; why are you alone?
Don't you know that you are My own?
Come near and let Me be your friend;
My love for you will never end.

"I want to stay where I am safe.
Outside my prison, it's not safe.
I do not trust Your words, so sweet.
I'd rather have no one to greet."

Come to Me; do not be afraid.
I won't plunder you or invade.
Help me to know just how you feel,
So I can help you to be real.

"I don't know if I can go.
Locked up inside is all I know.
I've tried before and failed, you see;
I do not know how to be me."

Come, My child, I call you to Me.
Your God, alone, can set you free.
As My life touches yours anew,
Won't you let Me partner with you?

Love, Jesus

"The Lord builds up Jerusalem; He gathers together the outcast of Israel. He heals the brokenhearted and binds up their wounds."

Psalm 147: 2-3

Chapter Four
A Darkened Abode

Loss of True Self

Defensive Hiding

- Forsaken sought to find a remedy for her distressful emotions.

- In the process, she hid from her *true self*.

_____

_____

_____

Live from your True Self

False Self: Mask

True Self

Hidden emotions, beliefs, desires, undeveloped abilities, unmet needs, need for God

Attitudes and behaviors intended to protect us from judgment and gain desired attention

Cherished / Forsaken

True Feelings
hurt
ashamed
anxious
fearful
angry
inadequate

False Persona
self-pity
acting out (running)
mistrust
withdrawn (defense)
needy
self hatred

True Identity
Mastery
Godly Desires
Creativity
Purity
Worth
Belonging
Trust

False Beliefs
Unfulfilled
Flesh Desires
Foolish Imaginations
Shame
Unworthiness
Outcast
Anxiety

Ignorance is not bliss!

Unattended pain and wounds can lead to:

- Defense mechanisms
- Misperceptions
- Over and under reacting
- Addictions and behaviors to numb the pain
- Self-destructive thoughts and actions
- Impure motivations
- Dysfunctional relationships

Hidden Motivations and Defenses

- In the natural, our psyche uses defense mechanisms to cope with internal and external stressors.

- These mechanisms, in and of themselves, are not bad.

- However, if left unchecked, they can lead to emotional illness and dysfunctional behavior.

_____

_____

_____

Defense Mechanisms

- Denial
- Splitting
- Displacement
- Projection
- Acting out behavior
- Obsessions & Compulsions
- Withdrawal
- Intellectualization
- Rationalization

Denial

Denial, repression, suppression:

- Conscious or subconscious anxiety forcing thoughts, feelings, attitudes, impulses and memories into the unconscious.

Splitting: Dissociation, depersonalization, emotional isolation, multiple personalities

- A segment of the individual's behavior is detached from consciousness in order to allow the expression of impulses or actions that are very threatening to the person.

Displacement

Anger

- The emotion (*usually anger*) is aroused toward one object and is transferred onto another object that is less threatening or dangerous to express the feeling toward.

_____

_____

_____

Projection

- Includes *blaming others* for one's own problems. In a fuller sense, it is attributing to another person one's own impulses, thoughts, feelings, attitudes and/or values that are felt to be too negative or threatening to accept into consciousness as aspects of the self.

Acting out behavior

- Anxiety and tension are reduced behaviorally

Anger

Addictions

Cycle of Addiction

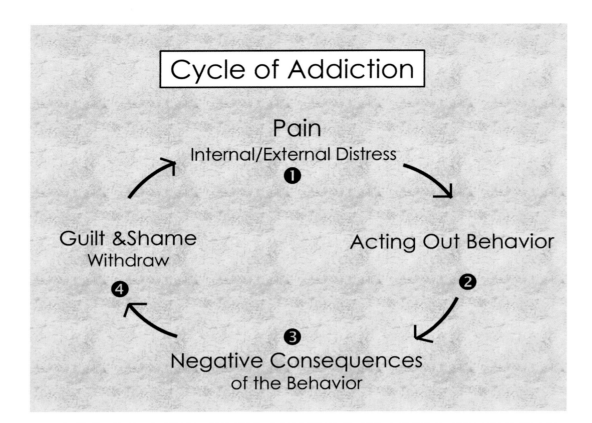

Pain
Internal/External Distress
❶

Acting Out Behavior
❷

Negative Consequences
of the Behavior
❸

Guilt &Shame
Withdraw
❹

Obsessions and Compulsions

- **Obsessions:**

Repetitive words, thoughts or daydreams that symbolically release energy from repressed impulses and conflicts. May sometimes increase anxiety when the content is destructive.

- **Compulsions:**

Repetitive behaviors that are often used to control anxiety.

_____

_____

_____

Withdrawal

Withdrawal:

- Either a physical or psychological movement out of or away from an extreme anxiety-producing situation.

Intellectualization and Rationalization

Intellectualization:

- The use of excessive talking, philosophical discussion and theoretical interpretations in order to avoid dealing with uncomfortable or threatening emotions.

Rationalization:

- This common *"excuse making"* response provides logical, rational explanations for one's behavior, which was probably motivated by unconscious and therefore irrational impulses and drives.

These are the ways that I am hiding my true self:

_____

_____

I use defenses in this way:

_____

_____

"For in Christ the fullness of God lives in a human body, and you are complete through your union with Christ."

Colossians 2:9-10 NLT

_____

_____

_____

The Awakening *by Graham Cooke*

Chapter Five
A Changed Heart

Gain a Change of Heart

- Choose to *believe* and trust in truth.

- Make a *choice* to yield to the Spirit.

- Soften your *heart* to receive healing.

_____

_____

_____

God's Deliberate Pursuit of Me

I cannot remember the date or the title of the pastor's message, but I vividly remember that he spoke directly into my spirit and soul. His words captivated my heart and stirred it awake from a long deep sleep. In some ways it was as though I was hearing those words for the first time in my life as this slightly built priest leaned over the pulpit and with magnetic force bellowed out, "Abba, your Father, has an extravagant love for you."

He measured out that phrase several more times with equal magnetism and I soon realized that the only thing my senses were attuned to was the pastor, Abba Father, and me. Time held no relevance; neither did the faces around me, nor the knowledge that chapel would soon be over and I would have to return to class. The only notable occurrence was that which was happening inside my own body, spirit and soul. Years of pain had programmed my heart not to feel, and now it was responding to the beckoning of the Spirit's call.

The breaking open of my heart was sweet. Abba (the Hebrew word for "Daddy") was befriending the heart that had turned from Him for so many years. It was my misperception that He had deserted me through my physical trials (like my childhood abandonment by my dad and grandma), when in reality, it was my heart that had grown inattentive. I paused in that holy moment and noticed that my heart was now turned toward Him— stilled by such an amazing extravagant love.

Will you turn your heart toward the Father today? His greatest gift came in the person of Jesus Christ who sacrificed His life for you. That is an extravagant love!

From *Meditations from the River* by Carol Romeo

Choose to believe and move towards the Spirit:

- God wants to be known.
- He is always relating to us *(even when we can't see)*.
- The Spirit was always with Cherished, waiting for her to be ready to hear Him.
- Communication breaks down because of:

  ego needs, misperceptions, unhealed wounds, self-protection (masks/defenses), failed expectations, lack of self-awareness, old habits and lies.

Wounded Heart Cycle

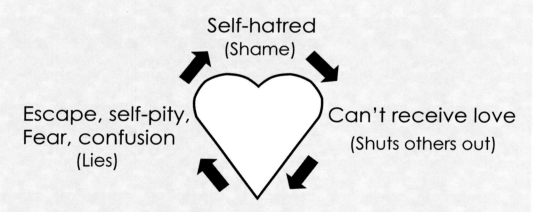

Self-hatred
(Shame)

Escape, self-pity,
Fear, confusion
(Lies)

Can't receive love
(Shuts others out)

Anger / Bitterness
(Perceived rejection from Life-Giver)

Cherished's Emotional State

True Feelings

- Hurt
- Ashamed
- Anxious
- Fearful
- Angry

Acted-Out Defensive Feelings

- Self-pity
- Mistrust
- Withdrawn
- Self-rejection
- Hopeless

Emotions are God Given

They serve a good purpose when they function in the way they were designed to function.

Healthy emotions alert us:

- Anger lets us know that someone has in some way harmed us. Anger says, "No, you will not do that to me again." Healthy anger sets a boundary with the other individual involved.

- Fear alerts us to danger. Fear says, "Stop what you are doing and pay attention to this!" Fear will activate our fight, flight or freeze response.

- All emotions tell us how we are feeling in a particular situation and can alert us to action.

Unhealthy emotions keep us stuck:

- Healthy emotions are fluid. An individual can move through the various circumstances of his/her life with relative ease and avoid remaining stuck in any one emotion.

- Emotions loose their natural fluidity, however, when we habitually react to them in unhealthy patterns (example: a victim stance or an aggressor stance).

- Self-awareness of our true emotions can bring us into health.

Come to the Lord Jesus with your...
Authentic Self

- Become *vulnerable*

- Uncover any shame

- Trust the *goodness* of God and

- His ability to impart that to you

Paul's prayer for spiritual empowering:

"I pray that from his glorious, unlimited resources he will give you mighty inner strength through his Holy Spirit. And I pray that Christ will be more and more at home in your hearts as you trust in him. May your roots go down deep into the soil of God's marvelous love. And may you have the power to understand, as all God's people should, how wide, how long, how high, and how deep his love really is...Then you will be filled with the fullness of life and power that comes from God."

Ephesians 3:16-18,19b NLT

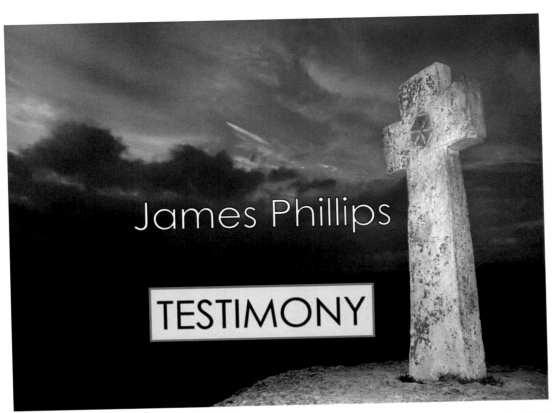

James Phillips

TESTIMONY

BODY, SOUL and SPIRIT

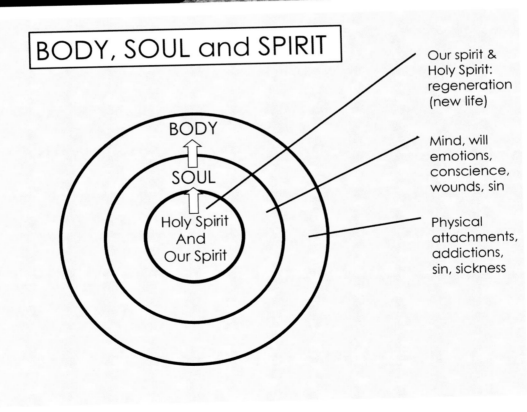

BODY

SOUL

Holy Spirit
And
Our Spirit

Our spirit &
Holy Spirit:
regeneration
(new life)

Mind, will
emotions,
conscience,
wounds, sin

Physical
attachments,
addictions,
sin, sickness

Act in conjunction with the Holy Spirit and not *react* out of your emotions or body!

Body *is* Leading	Soul *is* Leading	Spirit *is* Leading
BODY	SOUL	SPIRIT
↓	↓	↓
SOUL	BODY	SOUL
↓	↓	↓
SPIRIT	SPIRIT	BODY

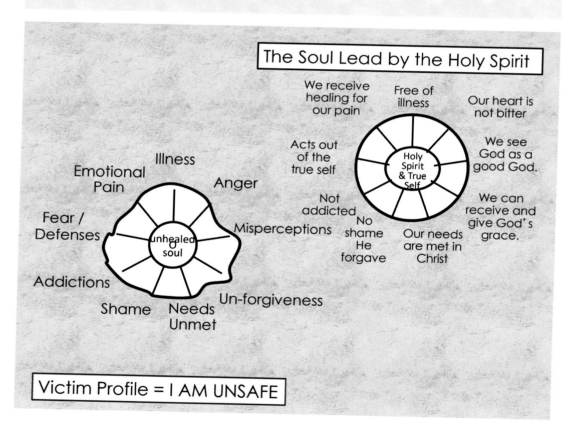

The Soul Lead by the Holy Spirit

We receive healing for our pain

Free of illness

Our heart is not bitter

Acts out of the true self

We see God as a good God.

Not addicted

No shame He forgave

Our needs are met in Christ

We can receive and give God's grace.

Holy Spirit & True Self

Illness

Emotional Pain

Anger

Fear / Defenses

Misperceptions

unhealed soul

Addictions

Shame

Needs Unmet

Un-forgiveness

Victim Profile = I AM UNSAFE

The Unburdened Soul: *Lead by the Holy Spirit*

Lie/Truth
Free of emotional
illness

Defense
Acts out
of
True Self

Holy
Spirit
& True
Self

Perception
We see God
as a good
God.

Expectation
Hope that
our needs are
met in Him

"Now may the God of peace Himself sanctify you completely; and may your whole *spirit, soul and body* be preserved blameless at the coming of our Lord Jesus Christ. He who calls you is faithful, who also will do it."

I Thessalonians 5:23-24

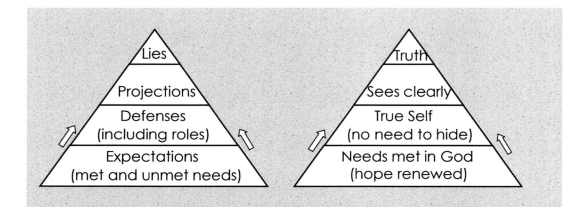

Which side do you find yourself on?

Where is your heart now?

- Perception of God: I can see God as a good God (0-10)

  _____

- Expectations: I know my need will be met in God (0-10)

  _____

- True Self: I am acting out of my true self (0-10)

  _____

- Lie/Truth: I am believing and living in truth (0-10)

  _____

_____

_____

_____

Chapter Six
A Way of Escape

Self-Examination

Cherished learned from Life-Giver…

"An altar is a place of surrender and a place of remembrance; surrender all to Me and you will gain life. And, remember that I will meet you there."

The distortions or lies we carry into today become the looking glass through which we see our world. Believing in these lies also opens the door for Satan's influence (who is known as the *father of lies*). Jesus spoke these words:

"...He was a murderer from the beginning and has always hated the truth. There is no truth in him. When he lies, it is consistent with his character; for he is a liar and the father of lies." (John 8:44b NLT)

"I can never escape from your spirit! I can never get away from your presence! If I go up to heaven, you are there; if I go down to the place of the dead, you are there. If I ride the wings of the morning, if I dwell by the farthest oceans, even there your hand will guide me, and your strength will support me. I could ask the darkness to hide me and the light around me to become night—but even in darkness I cannot hide from you. To you the night shines as bright as day. Darkness and light are both alike to you."

Psalm 139:7-12 NLT

My Night Terrors

Early in my Christian walk I would wake at night with fear gripping my soul. I didn't recognize what the fear was about; I just knew that I was filled with fear. *Terror* would actually be a better word because it was the kind of feeling that would grip my heart, shake me from my sleep and leave me motionless for hours, afraid to even whisper a prayer. I gradually learned how to battle my invisible foe by speaking the name of Jesus in my mind and forcing myself to get up and move into the living room. I had a plaque on the sofa table that contained the twenty-third psalm, and when I finally would be able to speak, I would read it aloud over and over. My ritual would continue for hours at a single setting and this practice extended over a period of several months.

Throughout this season of time the Holy Spirit began to illuminate the places in my soul that He desired to cleanse, and He gradually set me free from the bondage of my past. It was the baggage I was carrying that was kicking up all the fear. The enemy had owned me for many years, but now Jesus wanted to be my Lord. Every stronghold of the enemy had to be pulled down. Jesus desired to replace the fear with His love, and for this to happen I had to open my heart to Him in yet a deeper dimension. I had already received Jesus as my Savior, but there were areas of my heart that were still ruled by my flesh and the enemy. He wanted to be Lord of *all* that dwelled in my heart and being.

This is what He said,

Come, My child
Into the depths of My love.
Will it hurt? I asked of Him.
Sometimes, He said.
But, do you want to know Me?

Oh, yes, yes, I replied.
Come, take me to places
Even I have not seen.

But, I have seen them, He said.
And, they are not ugly to Me or shameful.
They are the jewels that will
Open the doors to My love.

But, Jesus, that doesn't make sense,
I told Him.
Those dark places seem *so* dark.

Child, dark is really light
Through My eyes.
Will you see what I see?
Will you hold the lantern of My Spirit
And walk down with Me into the hidden places?

I will, My Lord.
But, I need You to show me the way
And give me courage.
I will not fear if You are with me.

Yes, My child, yes
I will be with you.
But, will you choose to come?
I am calling to you.
Come to Me, come deeper, deeper still.

from: Meditations from the River by Carol Romeo

Place of surrender...

Jesus is faithful.
He will meet you there.

He has forgiveness for you!
He wants to give you His promise!
He wants to tell you the truth about
your significance!

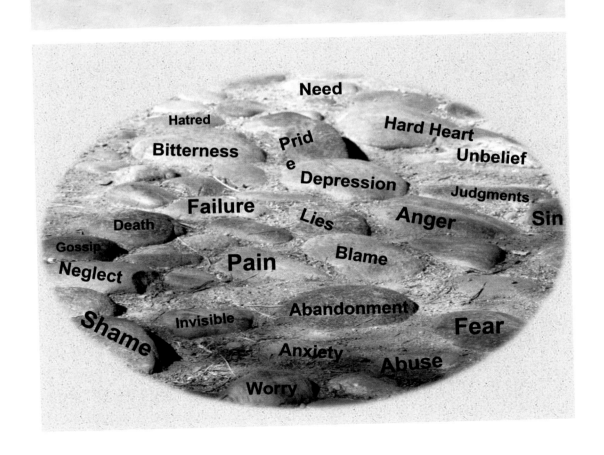

Self-examination: What are your stones?

- What wounds and grief are you holding on to and need to be healed of?

  _____

  _____

- What unmet needs and expectations do you want to bring to God?

  _____

  _____

- In what ways have you harmed or judged others or yourself?

  _____

  _____

- Are you carrying unbelief, lack of trust or not following the path God has set before you?

  _____

  _____

- What are the lies you have believed?

  _____

  _____

- What are the sins you need to repent of?

  _____

  _____

  _____

_____

_____

_____

Prayer

1. What lie has the enemy spoken about who you are and what you believe about yourself? ("I'm a failure. I'm worthless. I'm bad.")

2. Where did that lie begin? Holy Spirit would you reveal that truth right now? (It may be a childhood event or it may not.)

3. Pray: "Father, I know that You love me, but there is a part of me that hasn't received Your love fully. I can see a belief on the inside that pushes Your love away; a belief that I have to perform or prove my value to be loved. I recognize that there are events and people that helped me believe these things. As a result, I have cursed myself with my own perceptions and beliefs about me."

4. Are you willing to forgive yourself for believing the lie and any ways that you acted on that lie? Are you willing to release the judgments and curses?

5. Pray: "Jesus, you died so that I could be forgiven, but I have not received your forgiveness in those places where I have judged myself. I choose now to forgive myself and release myself from those judgments in the area of _____. I choose to have grace for me. Failure is an event, not a person. I am not a failure. I choose to believe what Christ says about me. (Listen to Him.)

6. Jesus, I choose to forgive and release any judgment against the following people _____ (those who have hurt or cursed me).

7. Now see yourself giving the people, offenses and pain to the Lord.

8. Pray: "Lord, show me how You see me. The way I have seen myself has been corrupted. Show me the self that You created." Wait.

9. Take your two hands and hold them out before you. In your left hand hold the damaged image of yourself (lie). In the right hand hold the image or truth that the Lord revealed to you.

10. Ask the Lord what He wants to do with the lie or the damaged image.

11. Invite Him to do it.

12. If the damaged self-perception were true, Satan would not have worked so hard to get you to believe it. Satan does not want you to walk in your destiny. Ask yourself, "Who is telling me the truth, Satan or Jesus?

13. Do you want to break agreement with Satan?

14. Pray: "Lord Jesus, thank You for showing me a little glimpse of who I am to You; how precious I am to You. Forgive me for believing the lies that kept me from that truth and the fullness of all You have for me. Today, by an act of my will, I now break the power of my agreement with Satan. I tear up the contract that I have made with my enemy when I spoke judgments and curses over myself. I declare that I am not _____ and _____.

By an act of my will, I take the authority that You, Jesus, gave me through the blood you shed for me and I say to the enemy that you hold no more power over me concerning the lies

_____.

15. Pray: "Thank you, Lord. Because of what You have done, I can see myself the way that You see me. Would You continue to breathe life into that image and, day by day, move me into the place of wholeness and the place of my destiny."

16. "And now I ask, Lord, that the eyes of my heart would see my true image and believe in the righteous destiny that You have for me, your child. Let the truth that You have released to me today go down deep into my heart, transforming my thoughts, feelings and actions. Thank you, Jesus. Amen"

Remember:
This is a spiritual journey

" Pay attention, my child, to what I say. Listen carefully. Don't lose sight of my words. Let them penetrate deep within your heart, for they bring life and radiant health to anyone who discovers their meaning. Above all else, guard your heart, for it affects everything you do."

Proverbs 4:20-23 NLT

_____

_____

_____

Chapter Seven
Walking in the Light

Hear the Spirit

As Forsaken yielded, once again, to the Spirit, she found:

- Renewed energy to move out of the cave and into the light.

- A new desire to embrace the promises she once discarded.

- Vision of her true identity and a desire to walk in it.

God Created Human Beings with Legitimate and Pure Needs and Longings

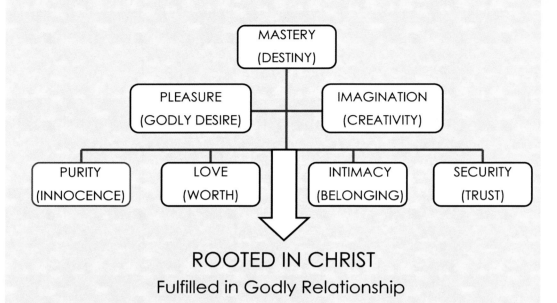

MASTERY
(DESTINY)

PLEASURE
(GODLY DESIRE)

IMAGINATION
(CREATIVITY)

PURITY
(INNOCENCE)

LOVE
(WORTH)

INTIMACY
(BELONGING)

SECURITY
(TRUST)

ROOTED IN CHRIST
Fulfilled in Godly Relationship

- Mastery
- Godly Desires
- Creativity
- Purity
- Worth
- Belonging
- Trust

What parts of your true identity, *(that you discarded)* do you want to now claim as you travel down your path? Be specific.

_____

_____

_____

_____

_____

_____

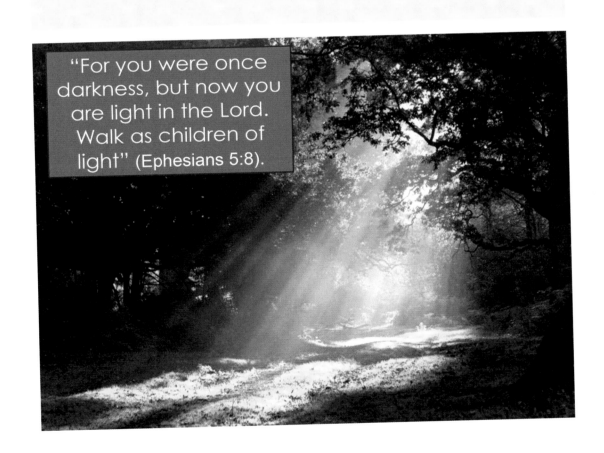

"For you were once darkness, but now you are light in the Lord. Walk as children of light" (Ephesians 5:8).

_____

_____

_____

- Fear and shame lifts
- Defenses drop
- Onset of new hope
- Return of self-esteem
- Desire to walk a new path

_____

_____

_____

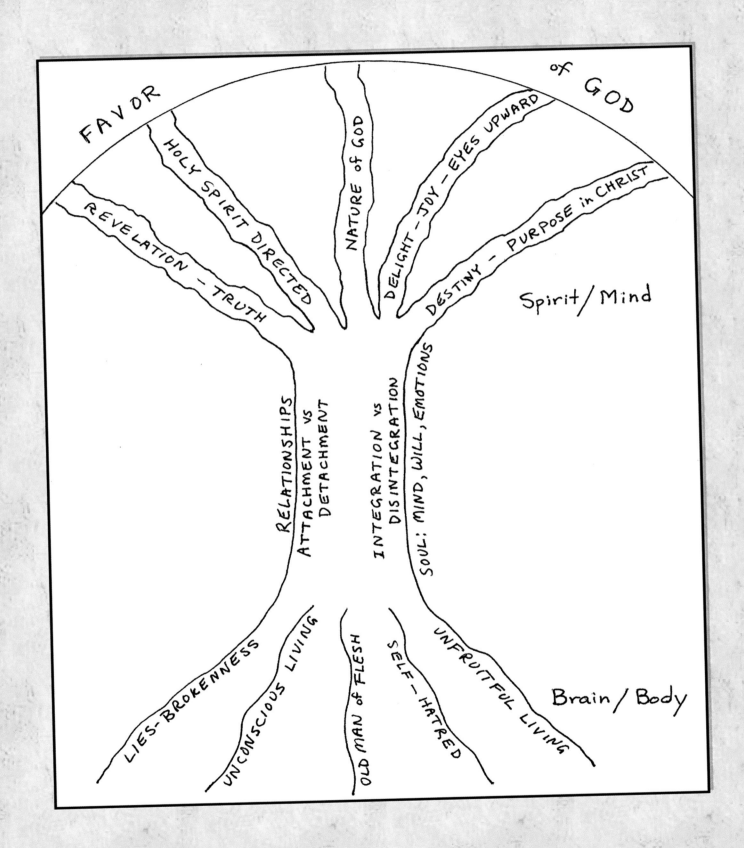

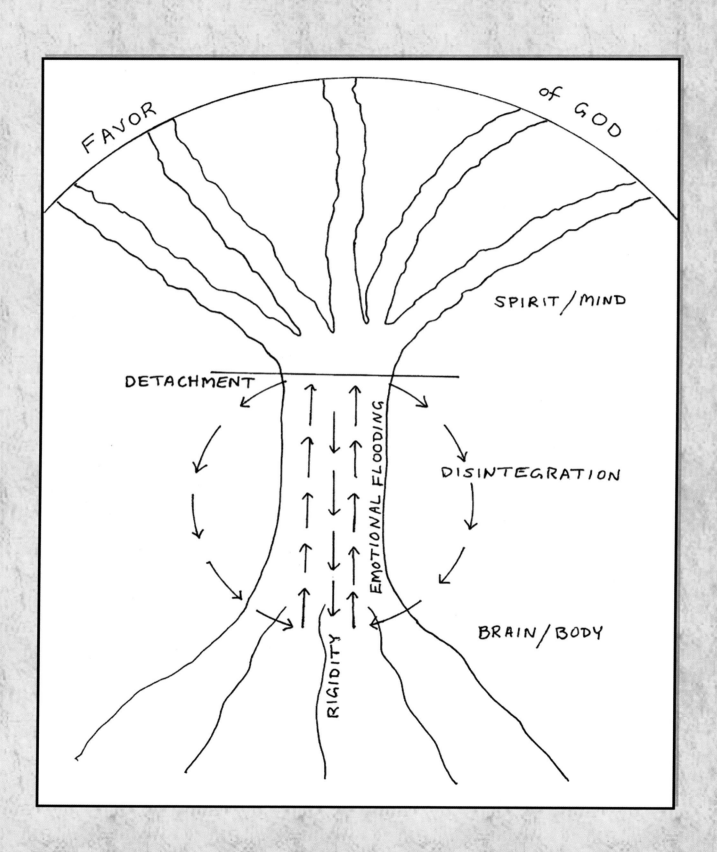

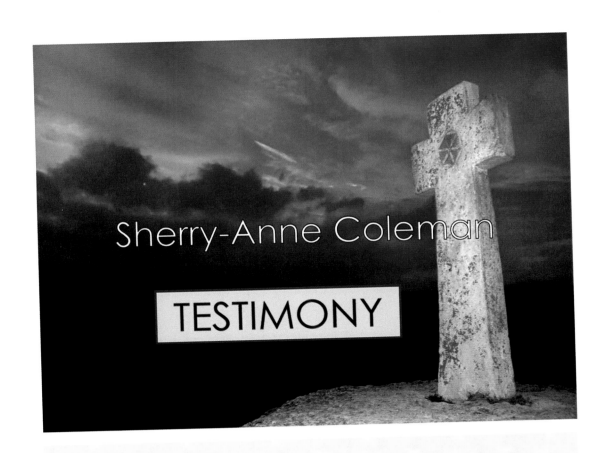

Sherry-Anne Coleman

TESTIMONY

Scripture References

- Psalm 139:13-17
- Psalm 27:10
- Jeremiah 29:11-13
- Hebrews 12:2
- Luke 19:10
- Isaiah 60:1
- 2 Corinthians 12:9

Chapter Eight
The Promise of Life

Yield to God

✝ As we travel with Jesus, our Life-Giver, we are given *courage* to fulfill our destiny to extend *His kingdom* of healing and life here on this earth.

_____
_____
_____
_____

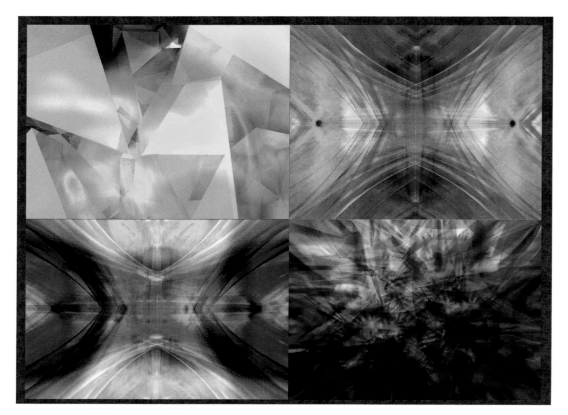

How big is your God?

The more we can see God in our circumstances, the bigger He becomes. Furthermore, the bigger He becomes, the bigger we become in our capacity to be like Him.

"Beloved, now we are children of God; and it has not yet been revealed what we shall be, but we know that when He is revealed, we shall be like Him, for we shall see Him as He is."

John 3:2

Stages of Growth

Expansive view of God / Growth or stagnation

⬆

Defensive response / Redemptive response

⬆

Central question (belief / lie)

⬆

Met / Unmet need (conflict)

⬆

Need / Expectation

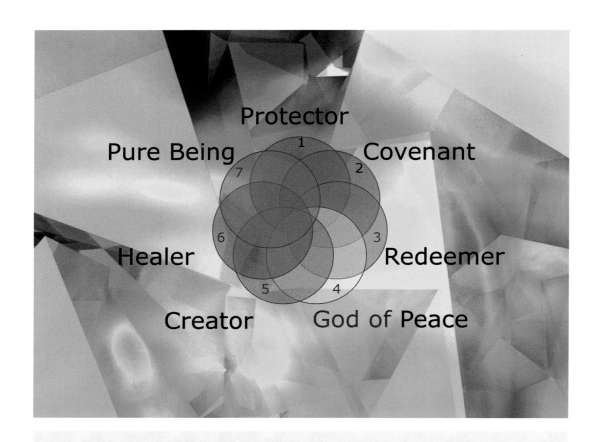

As you view each stage, pay attention to the following:

- Your need
- The internal conflict or stuck place
- A central question concerning the nature of God
- Names of God: How God is revealing Himself at that stage
- What responses did you have?

Stage One God: *Protector*

- **Need**: safety, survival

- **Conflict**: Is God re-warder or punisher?

- **Central Question**: In a world full of danger and chaos is God a good God?

- **Name of God**: Good Shepherd

John 10:11

Stages Adapted from: *How to Know God* by Deepak Chopra

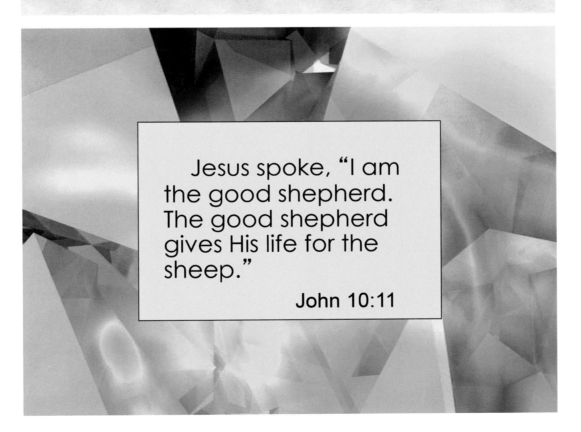

Jesus spoke, "I am the good shepherd. The good shepherd gives His life for the sheep."

John 10:11

Stage Two God: *Covenant*

- **Need**: belonging

- **Conflict**: worldly fulfillment or obedience to God

- **Central Question**: Is God a personal God? (Will God hear and answer MY prayers?)

- **Names of God**: Almighty (Gen. 17:1-2)

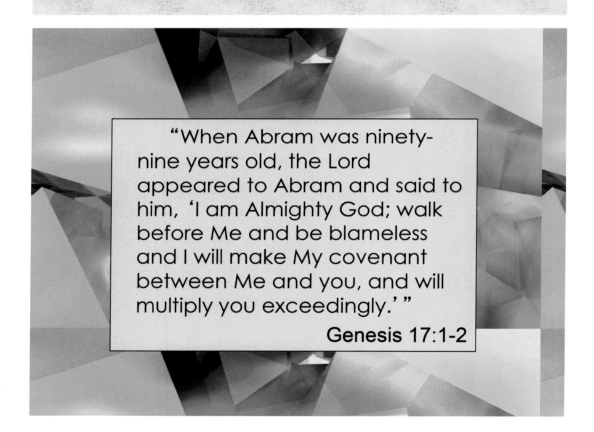

"When Abram was ninety-nine years old, the Lord appeared to Abram and said to him, 'I am Almighty God; walk before Me and be blameless and I will make My covenant between Me and you, and will multiply you exceedingly.'"

Genesis 17:1-2

Stage Three God: *Redeemer*

- **Need**: forgiveness of sins / worth

- **Conflict**: self-righteousness or shame vs. unconditional love

- **Central Question**: In my sin, will God be good to me?

- **Names of God**: Jesus the Savior (Matt. 1:21)

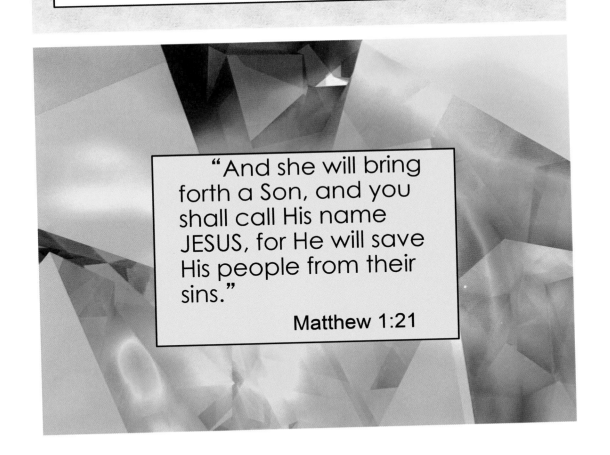

"And she will bring forth a Son, and you shall call His name JESUS, for He will save His people from their sins."

Matthew 1:21

Stage Four God: *Peace*

- **Need**: internal peace

- **Conflict**: anxiety vs. peace

- **Central Question**: How can I be in the world and not of it? (Is God able to keep me?)

- **Names of God**: Prince of Peace (Is.9:6)

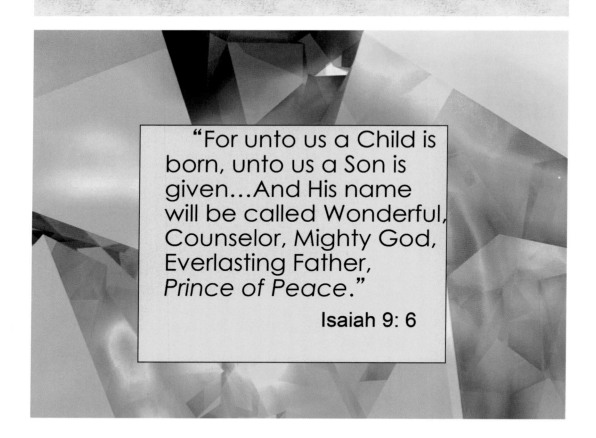

"For unto us a Child is born, unto us a Son is given...And His name will be called Wonderful, Counselor, Mighty God, Everlasting Father, *Prince of Peace.*"

Isaiah 9: 6

Stage Five God: *Creator*

- **Need**: to partner with God as co-creator in one's life

- **Conflict**: to align with God's will (destiny) vs. the ego intentions (self importance)

- **Central Question**: Does God want to communicate with me?

- **Name of God**: Creator (God created man in His image. We are the only members of creation who can reason with God).
Gen.1:1, 26-28

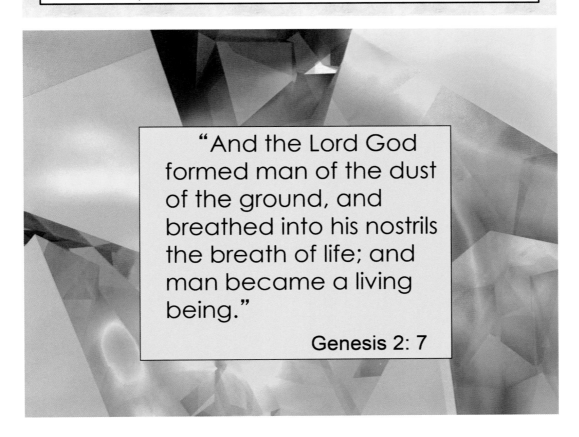

"And the Lord God formed man of the dust of the ground, and breathed into his nostrils the breath of life; and man became a living being."

Genesis 2: 7

Stage Six God: *Healer*

- **Need:** to experience God

- **Conflict:** the battle between seeing with our spiritual eyes (kingdom living) or trusting in the material world.

- **Central Question:** Is God a supernatural God? (Does He heal today?)

- **Name of God:** Physician (Jesus stood in the temple and declared Himself as physician.)

Lu. 4:16-24

Jesus (speaking of Himself) said, "The Spirit of the Lord is upon Me, because He has anointed Me to preach the gospel to the poor; He has sent Me to heal the brokenhearted, To proclaim liberty to the captives and recovery of sight to the blind..."

Luke 4: 18

_____

_____

_____

Stage Seven God: *Pure Being*

- **Need**: unity with God (transcendence) and unity with one another

- **Conflict**: how to transcend the limitations of humanity, time and space

- **Central Question**: How big is our God?

- **Name of God**: I AM (Ex. 3:14 & John 8:58)

"And God said to Moses, 'I AM WHO I AM.' And He said, 'Thus you shall say to the children of Israel, 'I AM has sent me to you.' "

Exodus 3:14

"Jesus said to them, 'Most assuredly. I say to you, before Abraham was, I AM.' "

John 8:58

God Created Human Beings with Legitimate and Pure Needs and Longings

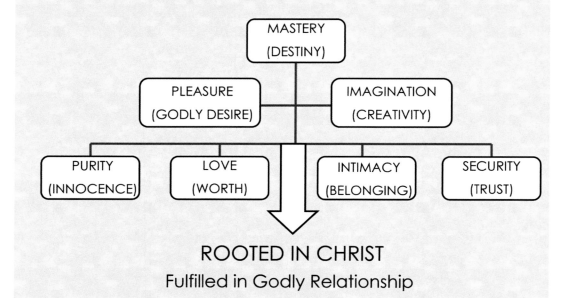

TRANSCENDENT SELF

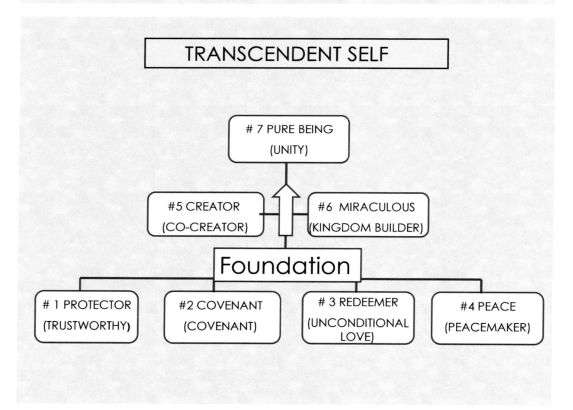

Jesus Prays for All Believers

"I am praying not only for these disciples but also for all who will ever believe in me because of their testimony. My prayer for all of them is that they will be one, just as you and I are one, Father—that just as you are in me and I am in you, so they will be in us, and the world will believe you sent me. I have given them the glory you gave me, so that they may be one, as we are—I in them and you in me, all being perfected into one. Then the world will know that you sent me and will understand that you love them as much as you love me."

John 17:20-23 NLT

Being Values

"Love is patient and kind. Love is not jealous or boastful or proud or rude. Love does not demand its own way. Love is not irritable, and it keeps no record of when it has been wronged. It is never glad about injustice but rejoices whenever the truth wins out. Love never gives up, never loses faith, is always hopeful, and endures through every circumstance."

1 Corinthians 13:4-8 NLT

> God has to stretch the foundation—
> that happens in **PROCESS**.

We can destroy in our character what we have built in our gifting.

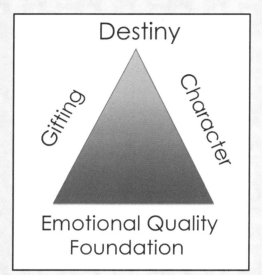

Destiny

Gifting

Character

Emotional Quality
Foundation

Being Values

- This is the fruit I see in my life:

  _____
  _____
  _____

- I am asking the Holy Spirit to produce this:

  _____
  _____
  _____

_____
_____
_____

Experiences with God

Loved church, liked vacation bible school (little lamb), holy communion (felt God's love), singing in the choir, liked the warm loving people

Conflict: Saw God as rewarder and punisher ⬇⬇

Received Christ (felt a loving presence), voice of God like thunder in church, filled with the Holy Spirit and manifestations, scripture popped out at me (calling), miraculous back healing, saved from death, supernatural bubble, freedom and deliverance

Age1-16	STAGE ONE	17 30: STAGE TWO	31-36: STAGE THREE/SIX

Need: Safety and Belonging (abandonment pain)

Need: Redeemer I needed God to rescue me from my sin, sadness and brokenness

Need: Forgiveness, emotional and physical healing. I experienced God within as well as the "bigness" of God.

Experiences with God

Need: Healing Expectation: For God to heal me the way He did previously

God proved faithful in His pursuit of me, reassured me in chapel of His love, brought me revelation concerning my destiny and the strength to achieve it, gradual physical healing, belonging to God renewed.

Miraculous visions, miraculous healing of depression, bodily sense of the Holy Spirit's presence, renewed unity with the Holy Spirit, greater peace in God.

37 42: STAGE ONE	43-50: STAGE TWO/THREE	51-56:STAGE SIX/FOUR

Conflict: Depression and physical illness brought me to a place of separation from God. I saw Him as punitive and unsafe.

Need: I had to return to stages TWO and THREE. God reminded me of His covenant promise to me and His ability to keep me even as He had saved me. ("I have kept you!")

Need: Emotional healing brought me a greater ability to take in God's love and assurance of His care.

Experiences with God

Need: Sought inner peace (in place of anxiety) and unity with God through contemplative prayer.	Need: God to transform some of the deeper motivations of my heart, give me a servant's heart, His will and timing not mine.
57-62: STAGES FOUR / FIVE / SEVEN	63-68: STAGE FIVE / SEVEN
I became co-creator with God throughout my writing experience. Although there were some very high moments, my greatest joy became the knowledge of His abiding presence (sometimes felt, but always known).	Even though there was a crisis event in my life, I was able to sustain and deepen the internal peace and gain a greater sense of unity with God.

Your Experience

1. Make a list of your experiences with God.

2. Explore the emotional or situational event that preceded and followed each experience.

3. Identify the internal conflict or question concerning the character of God.

4. Make a chart showing the stage of God experienced for each age.

5. What have you learned about yourself?

6. What have you learned about God?

"And as you go, preach, saying, 'the kingdom of heaven is at hand.' Heal the sick, cleanse the lepers, raise the dead, cast out demons. *Freely you have received, freely give.*"

Matthew 10:7-8

_____

_____

_____

Printed in the United States
By Bookmasters